DISCOVERING Space

THE NEAR PLANETS

Ian Graham

W
FRANKLIN WATTS

(A) An Appleseed Editions book

First published in 2007 by Franklin Watts

Franklin Watts
338 Euston Road, London NW1 3BH

Franklin Watts Australia
Level 17/207 Kent St, Sydney, NSW 2000

© 2007 Appleseed Editions

Appleseed Editions Ltd
Well House, Friars Hill, Guestling, East Sussex TN35 4ET

Created by Q2A Media
Series Editor: Honor Head
Designers: Diksha Khatri, Ashita Murgai
Picture Researchers: Lalit Dalal, Jyoti Sachdev

ISBN   978 0 7496 7547 9

Dewey classification: 523.4

All words in **bold** can be found in the glossary on page 30.

A CIP catalogue for this book is available from the British Library.

Picture credits
t=top b=bottom c=centre l=left r=right m=middle
Cover images: Nasa: t, ml, mr, Science Photo Library/ Photolibrary: b
Small images: Science Photo Library/ Photolibrary: ml, Calvin J. Hamilton: cml, Nasa: cmr, mr.
Nasa/ JPL-Caltech: 4t, 5t, 19t, Science Photo Library/ Photolibrary: 4b, 6b, 7t, 9t, 9b, 11b, 12 (background), 16b,
17 (background), 20b, 21t, 27m, Nasa: 5b, 12b, 14t, 15b, 21b, 25t, 26-27 (background), 26b,
Jurgen Ziewe/ Shutterstock: 7b, Nasa Copyright Free Policy: 8b, 22m, ESA - AOES Medialab: 10-11(background), Calvin J.
Hamilton: 10b, Corbis: 13t, Earth Observatory/ Nasa: 14-15(background), Pacific Stock/ Photolibrary: 17b, U.S. Space & Rocket
Center: 18-19(background), JPL/ Nasa: 18b, Peter Arnold Images Inc/ Photolibrary: 23b, ESA: 24 (background), 24b.

Printed in China

Franklin Watts is a division of Hachette Children's Books

Contents

The near planets

Some **planets** are small and rocky, others are giant gas planets. The four planets nearest to the Sun belong to the group of small rocky planets. They are Mercury, Venus, Earth and Mars.

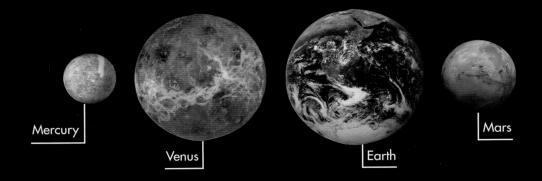

Mercury

Venus

Earth

Mars

Hot rocks

These four planets are called the near planets. They formed at the same time as the Sun. They were so hot to begin with that they melted. Over millions of years the heat slowly escaped into space. As each planet cooled down, its surface hardened to a rocky **crust**.

Meteorites crashed into the young Earth when it was forming.

Surrounded by gas

Most of the near planets are surrounded by a mixture of gases called an **atmosphere**. A planet's **gravity** holds the atmosphere in place around the planet. The bigger the planet, the stronger its gravity. Venus and Earth are the biggest of the near planets. They have the strongest gravity and the thickest atmospheres. Mars is smaller, so it has a very thin atmosphere. Mercury is the smallest of the near planets. Its gravity is too weak to hold on to an atmosphere so it has almost none.

White clouds of water droplets swirl around in the Earth's atmosphere.

The Earth's Moon is the biggest **moon** orbiting any of the four near planets.

Spotlight on
space

The eight planets of the Solar System have more than 150 moons, but only three of these moons orbit the four near planets. Mercury and Venus have no moons. Earth has one big moon. Mars has two tiny moons.

Mercury

Mercury is the smallest of the near planets and is the planet closest to the Sun. It is not much bigger than the Earth's Moon and if you could see it close up it would look like the Moon, too.

Hot and cold

Mercury is so close to the Sun that the side facing the Sun is heated to 400 degrees Celsius. That is four times as hot as boiling water. The side facing away from the Sun plunges to -200 degrees Celsius, which is a long way below freezing.

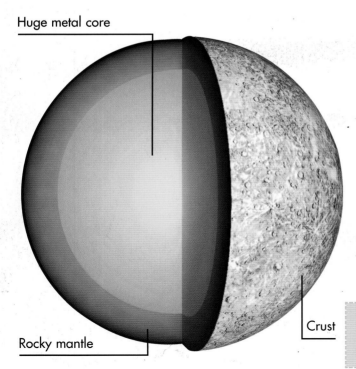

Huge metal core

Rocky mantle

Crust

Mercury facts

Size across the middle	▶	4,878 kilometres
Distance from the Sun	▶	58 million kilometres
Gravity	▶	about one third the strength of Earth's
Atmosphere	▶	none
Moons	▶	none
Length of day	▶	176 Earth days
Length of year	▶	88 Earth days

For such a small planet, Mercury has a huge metal **core**.

Mercury is covered with craters caused by rocks from space crashing into it.

The largest feature on the surface of Mercury is a vast crater called the Caloris Basin. It was made when a giant rock hit Mercury. The crater is 1,350 kilometres across. That makes it one of the biggest craters anywhere in the Solar System. A crater this big is also called an impact basin. When the rock hit Mercury, the ground on the other side of the planet bent and cracked. Scientists call it the Weird Terrain.

Spotlight on space

Although Mercury travels around the Sun very quickly, it spins very slowly. This means that a day on Mercury is twice as long as a year on Mercury.

Mercury travels around the Sun four times faster than Earth does.

Mercury

Sun

Exploring Mercury

Mercury is a difficult planet to explore because it is so close to the Sun. A **space probe** visiting Mercury has to be able to survive the Sun's scorching heat. Mercury has been visited by only one space probe so far, but another is on the way.

Spotlight on
space

The Messenger space probe will orbit Mercury. It will take photographs of the whole planet. Its instruments will study the planet from as close as 200 kilometres.

Mariner 10

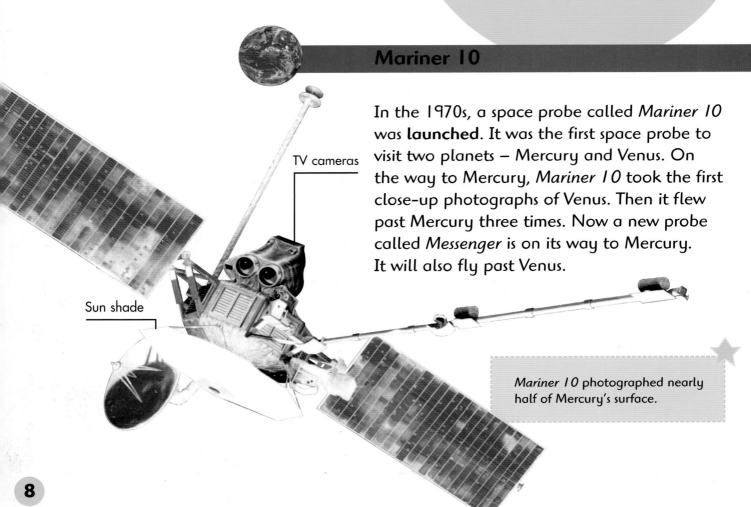

TV cameras

Sun shade

In the 1970s, a space probe called *Mariner 10* was **launched**. It was the first space probe to visit two planets – Mercury and Venus. On the way to Mercury, *Mariner 10* took the first close-up photographs of Venus. Then it flew past Mercury three times. Now a new probe called *Messenger* is on its way to Mercury. It will also fly past Venus.

Mariner 10 photographed nearly half of Mercury's surface.

BepiColombo

A new space mission to Mercury called *BepiColombo* will begin in the year 2013. It is named after a space scientist called Giuseppe (Bepi) Colombo. He was the scientist who suggested sending the *Mariner 10* space probe past Venus on its way to Mercury. Two *BepiColombo* space probes will be launched to study Mercury in more detail.

The *Messenger* space probe will spend a year in orbit around Mercury.

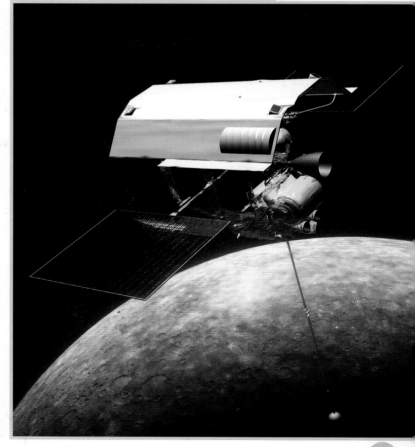

Messenger mission

Launched	▶	3 August 2004
Earth fly-by	▶	2 August 2005
First Venus fly-by	▶	24 October 2006
Second Venus fly-by	▶	6 June 2007
First Mercury fly-by	▶	15 January 2008
Second Mercury fly-by	▶	6 October 2008
Third Mercury fly-by	▶	30 September 2009

Venus

Venus is the second planet from the Sun and the closest to Earth. It is about the same size as Earth but it is a very different planet. If you stood on its surface you would be roasted, crushed and poisoned, all at the same time.

Hothouse planet

The surface of Venus is always hidden under the planet's thick atmosphere. So much of the Sun's heat is trapped by the atmosphere that the temperature soars to 480 degrees Celsius. That is hotter than Mercury. The atmosphere is so thick that it presses down nearly 100 times more than the Earth's atmosphere. This would crush any human being immediately.

Venus facts

Size across the middle	▶	12,104 kilometres
Distance from the Sun	▶	108 million kilometres
Gravity	▶	nearly the same strength as Earth's
Atmosphere	▶	mostly carbon dioxide
Moons	▶	none
Length of day	▶	117 Earth days
Length of year	▶	225 Earth days

The clouds on Venus contain **sulphuric acid** which burns and chokes.

Wrong spin

Venus spins more slowly than any other planet and it spins in the wrong direction. On Earth the Sun rises in the east every morning, on Venus the Sun rises in the west. Venus spins so slowly that there are less than two Venus days in a Venus year. When the planets formed, they were all spinning in the same direction and no one knows why Venus changed. Some scientists think it might have been hit by a giant space rock which caused it to start spinning in the opposite direction.

A volcano erupting on Venus's surface might look like this.

The *Venera 9* lander could stay on the surface of Venus for only two hours because of the atmosphere and heat.

Spotlight on
space

Scientists got their first view of the surface of Venus in 1975. The Russian space probe Venera 9 sent a lander craft down to the surface. It took one picture. This showed flat slabs of rocks scattered all over the surface.

Mapping Venus

To find out more about Venus scientists had to design and build a **spacecraft** that could see through the thick clouds around the planet and make maps of its surface. The result was the *Pioneer Venus*, sent to Venus in 1978.

Seeing the surface

Part of its mission was to make maps of the surface of the planet while cameras and instruments on board recorded other information. Then, in 1989, a bigger and better spacecraft called *Magellan* was sent to Venus.

Colours have been added to this map of Venus. Yellow shows the highest ground, blue the lowest.

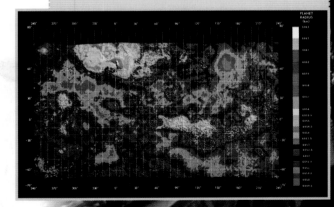

The *Magellan* spacecraft was launched by a **space shuttle**.

space

The two spacecraft, Pioneer Venus and Magellan, fired radio waves through Venus's thick clouds. The radio waves bounced off the planet and the spacecraft used the reflected waves to work out the shape of the surface.

The *Magellan* space probe spent four years orbiting Venus and mapping its surface. The information was beamed to Earth by radio.

Under the clouds

Scientists thought Venus might look like Earth but without water or life. However, the probes revealed that, in fact, Venus has a huge number of volcanoes. There are also not as many craters as scientists had expected. Scientists think **lava** from Venus's many volcanoes must have flooded out across the planet's surface and covered up most of the old craters. The *Magellan* space probe was eventually dragged into Venus's atmosphere and destroyed.

Magellan mission

Launched	▶ 5 May 1989
Arrived at Venus	▶ 10 August 1990
Mapping began	▶ 15 September 1990
Spacecraft destroyed	▶ 13 October 1994

Earth – our home planet

Earth is the third planet from the Sun and the biggest of the four near planets. It is the only planet known to have life. Earth has one moon, called the Moon, which we can see in the sky at night.

Nearly three–quarters of the Earth's surface is covered with water.

Earth facts

Size across the middle	▶	12,756 kilometres
Distance from the Sun	▶	150 million kilometres
Gravity	▶	one-G
Atmosphere	▶	mainly nitrogen and oxygen
Moons	▶	1
Length of day	▶	24 hours
Length of year	▶	365.25 days

Water world

Earth is like a colourful ball floating in the blackness of space. Its surface is covered by blue oceans, green and brown land and white **ice caps**. It is the only planet with oceans and seas. Water, and heat from the Sun, made it possible for life to develop on Earth.

Earth's seasons

The Earth tilts like a spinning top leaning over. When the top half of the Earth tilts towards the Sun, it is summer in northern Europe and North America. When it is summer in the north, it is winter in the south. As the Earth moves along its orbit to the other side of the Sun, it tilts away from the Sun. The land and the air above it cool down and the season changes from summer to autumn and then to winter.

The Earth is a planet of vast oceans and islands, clouds and rain, volcanoes and mountains.

The same side of the Moon always faces the Earth.

Spotlight on
space

Of all the moons orbiting the planets, only four other moons are bigger than ours. Three of these belong to Jupiter and are called Io, Ganymede and Callisto. One belongs to Saturn and is called Titan.

From core to crust

The Earth is not the same all the way through. When it formed, the heaviest materials sank to the centre and formed the Earth's core. Lighter materials floated on top of the core.

Metal and rock

The Earth's core is made of metal, mainly iron. The centre is solid, but the outer part of the core is liquid metal. The core is surrounded by a hot, slowly flowing rock called the mantle. This is covered by a thin crust of solid rock. We live on top of the crust.

The centre of the Earth is as hot as the surface of the Sun.

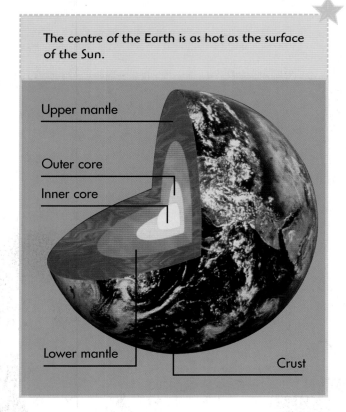

Upper mantle

Outer core

Inner core

Lower mantle

Crust

Inside the Earth

Inner core	▶	2,780 kilometres across
Outer core	▶	about 2,050 kilometres thick
Mantle	▶	about 2,890 kilometres thick
Crust	▶	about 50 kilometres thick

Missing craters

Earth is close to the Moon so it must have been hit by as many space rocks as the Moon. But the Moon is covered with thousands of craters and Earth has very few. The weather, water, earthquakes and volcanoes have changed the Earth's surface so most of the craters made on Earth have slowly disappeared.

The San Andreas fault in California, USA, is a long crack in the ground where two of the Earth's crust **plates** meet.

Spotlight on
space

The Earth's crust is like a cracked eggshell. It is made of slowly moving plates of rock. Some of them push into each other, some rub against each other and others pull apart. This can cause earthquakes and volcanoes.

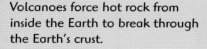

Volcanoes force hot rock from inside the Earth to break through the Earth's crust.

Mars – the red planet

Mars is known as the red planet because it is covered with rust-red dust. In many ways it is like Earth – it has ice caps at its north and south **poles** and it tilts, so it has seasons like Earth.

Looking for water

On 10 March 2006, a space probe called *Mars Reconnaissance Orbiter* was sent into orbit around Mars. It is sending back the clearest pictures of Mars ever taken and it is looking for signs of water. It joined three other spacecraft in orbit around Mars – *Mars Global Surveyor*, *Mars Odyssey* and *Mars Express*.

Mars facts

Size across the middle	▶	6,786 kilometres
Distance from the Sun	▶	228 million kilometres
Gravity	▶	about one third of the strength of Earth's
Atmosphere	▶	mainly carbon dioxide
Moons	▶	2
Length of day	▶	about 40 minutes longer than an Earth day
Length of year	▶	687 Earth days

From space, the *Mars Reconnaissance Orbiter's* cameras can see rocks as small as 20 centimetres across on the surface of Mars.

Spotlight on
space

The biggest volcano in the Solar System is on Mars. It is called Olympus Mons. It is 24 kilometres high, nearly three times the height of Mount Everest, the tallest mountain on Earth.

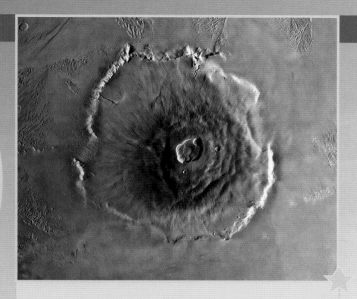

Olympus Mons is a giant volcano on Mars. It could be as much as 200 million years old.

Moons

Mars has two small moons called Phobos and Deimos. Phobos is the larger moon, but its diameter is only 27 kilometres. It orbits just 6,000 kilometres above Mars, so it is about 60 times closer to Mars than our Moon is to Earth. Phobos is slowly moving even closer to Mars and in 50 million years it will crash into the surface. The other moon, Deimos, has a diameter of only 15 kilometres. Both moons may be space rocks which were trapped by Mars' gravity.

This crater on Mars is called Endurance. It was formed by a rock from space crashing into the planet.

Life on Mars

More than a hundred years ago some **astronomers** thought they could see lines on the surface of Mars. They wondered if these lines might be canals built by **Martians** to move water around the planet.

Visiting Mars

The *Mariner 4* space probe flew past Mars in 1965. It took the first close-up photographs of the planet. There were no canals and no Martian cities in the pictures. Today, scientists believe the lines were an optical illusion, possibly created by drifting Mars dust.

Spotlight on
space

In 1976, two spacecraft called Viking 1 and Viking 2 landed on Mars to study the weather. They also scooped up some soil and tested it for signs of life but the tests found nothing.

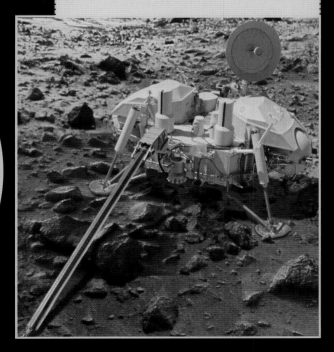

The two *Viking* spacecraft that landed on Mars took spectacular photographs of the planet's surface.

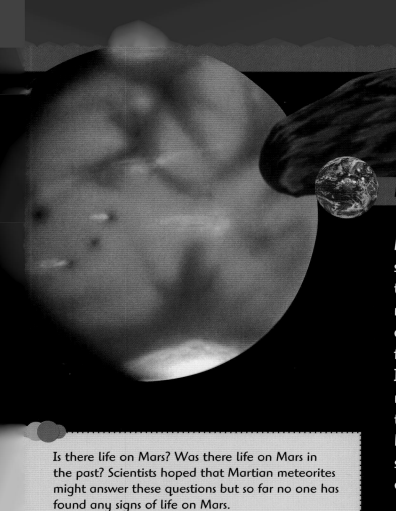

Mars worms?

Mars has been hit by big rocks from space many times in the past. When they landed they sent lots of Mars rocks flying up and some of these flew all the way into space. Amazingly, a few of these rocks landed on Earth. In 1996, scientists examined a Mars rock called ALH84001. They found tiny worm-like objects that might have been alive on Mars in the past. Other scientists think this is not possible and are still not sure what these objects are.

Is there life on Mars? Was there life on Mars in the past? Scientists hoped that Martian meteorites might answer these questions but so far no one has found any signs of life on Mars.

Some of the first maps of Mars showed canals criss-crossing the planet, but they did not exist.

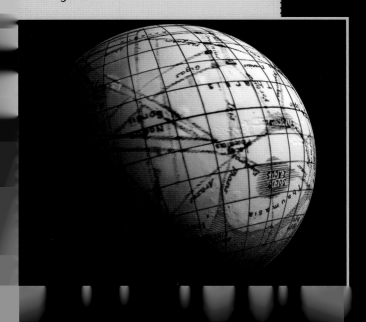

Viking missions

Viking 1 launched	▶	20 August 1975
Viking 2 launched	▶	9 September 1975
Viking 1 landed on Mars	▶	20 July 1976
Viking 2 landed on Mars	▶	3 September 1976

Robot explorers

By 2006, about a dozen spacecraft had either crashed into Mars or landed safely. Three of the spacecraft were **rover vehicles**, which moved across the surface of Mars studying the rocks and soil. They took thousands of photographs and sent weather reports back to Earth.

Mars rovers

Two Mars exploration rovers landed safely on opposite sides of the planet at the beginning of 2004. One was called *Spirit* and the other was called *Opportunity*. Scientists on Earth could move them by remote control and sent them out to explore the planet's surface and to collect information.

A Mars exploration rover drives across the rocky Martian surface.

Mars exploration rover mission

		Spirit	Opportunity
Launched	▶	10 June 2003	7 July 2003
Landed on Mars	▶	4 January 2004	25 January 2004
Landing site	▶	Gusev crater	Meridiani terra

A day on Mars

Every day *Spirit* and *Opportunity* are given their instructions by scientists on Earth. When one of the rovers reaches an interesting rock, its arm stretches out to scrape away the surface and reveal the rock underneath. It then sends the photographs and other information it has gathered back to Earth, where the next day's work is planned. Each rover was expected to last for about three months, but both were still working more than two years later, in the middle of 2007.

The surface of Mars is covered with red rocks and dust. Strong winds sometimes create dust storms.

Manned missions

Only robots have landed on Mars so far but there are now plans to send astronauts to the red planet. People could be walking on Mars for the first time before the end of the 21st century. Mars will be the first planet to be visited by astronauts.

A Mars base may be built near the South Pole.

This is an artist's impression of what spacecraft to Mars might look like.

Aurora – the first mission

The European Space Agency has a plan called *Aurora* to send astronauts to the Moon and then to Mars. At first they plan to send just robots. If this stage is successful, the ESA will then decide if they want to send astronauts.

Going to Mars

There are several other plans for landing people on Mars. One of these begins by sending an unmanned spacecraft to Mars ahead of the astronauts with enough fuel to bring the astronauts home at the end of the mission. Or, a spacecraft might land empty on Mars and make enough fuel for the trip home from gas in the Martian atmosphere. Scientists need to be sure they have a way of getting the astronauts back to Earth before they send them to Mars. The astronauts would spend 18 months exploring Mars.

Astronauts will need spacesuits on Mars because there is not enough **oxygen** in the atmosphere to breathe.

Spotlight on space

Before astronauts go to Mars, everything they use will be tested in 'Mars' bases built on Earth. These bases will copy the way life would be on Mars. Any problems can then be corrected before the Mars missions.

Aurora timeline

2011	▶	A rover called *Exo-Mars* will be sent to Mars
2014	▶	Equipment and craft will be tested for a manned landing on Mars
2016	▶	An unmanned mission will be sent to bring Mars rocks back to Earth
2018	▶	Engines and landing systems will be tested for a manned mission to Mars
2024	▶	A manned mission will go to the Moon
2026	▶	An unmanned test-flight to Mars
2030-33	▶	The first manned mission to Mars

Living on Mars

The first manned space missions to Mars will land astronauts on the planet for a few months and then bring them back to Earth. But one day, the red planet could become a second home for humans.

Changing Mars

Some scientists think Mars can be changed to make it more like Earth. A thicker atmosphere would stop some of the harmful **radiation** reaching the ground. It would also soak up more of the Sun's energy and increase the temperature on Mars. Oxygen would have to be added for people to breathe. If this could be done, people would be able to live on Mars without wearing spacesuits.

Spotlight on
space

Dangerous radiation from space travels through the Martian atmosphere all the way down to the ground. One way people might protect themselves from radiation is by living under the surface of the planet.

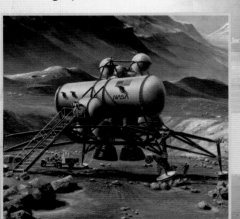

The first buildings on Mars will be built from parts of rockets and spacecraft linked together.

Living off the planet

Making a planet more like Earth is called **terraforming**. The first people to live on Mars will have to bring everything they need with them from Earth. But if terraforming is successful, eventually humans will be able to make all they need on the planet. They will be able to make bricks for building from the Martian soil; they will produce oxygen to breathe from the Martian atmosphere and they will grow vegetables and plants under huge domes.

Living on Mars

► Mars is colder than Earth

► Gravity is weaker than on Earth

► The seasons are twice as long as on Earth

► The days are about the same length as on Earth

One day, people might live inside domes on Mars. The domes will hold in air and keep out radiation.

Making Mars a place suitable for humans to live will take many years.

Timeline

3000 BC
The Babylonians describe Mercury in their writings.

240 BC
The Greek astronomer and poet Eratosthenes measures the size of the Earth.

1609
The English mathematician Thomas Harriott draws the first map of the Moon with the help of a telescope.

1639
Venus is seen crossing in front of the Sun.

1659
Markings are seen on the surface of Mars for the first time.

1666
Polar ice caps are seen on Mars for the first time.

1761
Venus's atmosphere is discovered.

1877
The Italian astronomer Giovanni Schiaparelli sees lines on Mars and calls them 'canali', meaning canals.

1959
The Russian space probe *Luna 1* is the first to fly past the Moon.

Luna 2 is the first probe to crash on to the Moon.

Luna 3 is the first probe to photograph the far side of the Moon.

1962
Mariner 2 flies past Venus.

1965
Mariner 4 takes close-up photographs of Mars.

1966
The Russian space probe, *Luna 9*, makes the first controlled landing on the Moon.

The US space probe *Surveyor 1* lands on the Moon.

1969
Apollo 11 makes the first manned landing on the Moon.

1970
The Russian space probe *Venera 7* makes the first controlled landing on Venus.

1971
US space probe *Mariner 9* goes into orbit around Mars.

1972
Apollo 17 makes the last manned landing on the Moon in the 20th century.

1973
Mariner 10 is launched on a mission to Mercury.

1974
Mariner 10 flies past Venus in February and flies past Mercury in March and again in September.

1975
Venera 9 and *Venera 10* land on Venus and send back the first pictures taken from its surface.

1975
Mariner 10 flies past Mercury for the third and last time.

1976
Viking 1 and *Viking 2* land on Mars.

1978
The *Pioneer* space probe is launched on a mission to Venus.

1989
The *Magellan* space probe is launched to make detailed maps of Venus.

1991
Galileo flies past Venus on its way to Jupiter.

1996
The *Lunar Prospector* space probe detects water on the Moon.

The *Mars Pathfinder* mission is launched to Mars.

1997
Mars Pathfinder lands on Mars and unloads a small robot rover called *Sojourner* to explore the surface.

Mars Global Surveyor goes into orbit around Mars.

1998
Cassini flies past Venus on its way to Saturn.

The *Mars Climate Orbiter* space probe is launched.

1999
The *Mars Climate Orbiter* is destroyed when it flies too close to Mars.

2001
Mars Odyssey goes into orbit around Mars.

2002
Mars Odyssey begins mapping the surface of Mars and searching for water.

2003
The British Mars lander *Beagle 2* arrives at Mars, but no radio signal is received from it.

The Mars exploration rovers *Spirit* and *Opportunity* are launched.

2004
The Mars exploration rovers *Spirit* and *Opportunity* land on Mars.

The *Messenger* space probe is launched on its way to Mercury.

2005
The US space probe *Mars Reconnaissance Orbiter* is launched.

The European space probe *Venus Express* is launched.

2006
Mars Reconnaissance Orbiter goes into orbit around Mars.

Venus Express goes into orbit around Venus.

2007
The *Phoenix* Mars lander is due to be launched to Mars.

2011
The *Messenger* space probe is due to go into orbit around Mercury.

2013
The two space probes of the *BepiColombo* space mission are due to be launched to Mercury.

2019
BepiColombo is due to arrive at Mercury.

Glossary

astronomers Scientists who study astronomy — the stars, moons and planets.

atmosphere The gas around a planet or moon. The Earth's atmosphere is made of air.

core A planet's core is its centre. The four near planets have cores made of metal, mainly iron.

crater A shallow circular dip in the surface of a planet or moon caused by a space rock smashing into it.

crust The rocky surface layer of a planet or a satellite like the Moon.

gravity An invisible force that pulls things towards each other. Earth's gravity pulls us down on to the ground and keeps the Moon in orbit around the Earth.

ice caps Frozen water covering the poles of a planet.

impact basin A huge crater, bigger than about 300 kilometres across, caused by a giant rock hitting a planet or moon.

lander craft A spacecraft designed to land on other planets.

launched When a spacecraft takes off at the beginning of its spaceflight.

lava The hot liquid rock that pours out of a volcano.

mantle A layer of rock below the Earth's crust and above the core.

Martians People from Mars. It has now been proved that there are no people in Mars.

meteorites Rocks that fall on to a planet from space.

moon A small object orbiting a planet. The Earth has one moon, called the Moon.

one-G The force of gravity on the surface of the Earth.

orbit To move around the Sun as a planet does, or to move around a planet as a satellite like the moon does around the Earth.

oxygen A gas in the air which is needed for survival by most of the life on Earth.

planets Very big objects in space which orbit a star.

plates Huge pieces of rock that make up the Earth's crust. They are constantly moving very slowly. Sometimes they bump into each other, causing an earthquake.

poles Two points at the furthest north and south of a planet.

radiation Particles or waves given out by something. Solar radiation is made up of the particles and waves given out by the Sun.

radio waves Energy waves like light waves but made of longer waves.

reconnaissance Watching or studying closely. The *Mars Reconnaissance Orbiter* is a space probe designed to watch Mars closely.

rover vehicles Robot or radio-controlled vehicles that move around on the surface of a planet.

Solar System The Sun, planets, moons and everything else that orbits the Sun.

spacecraft A machine sent into space. Manned spacecraft have people inside. Unmanned spacecraft have no one inside.

space probe An unmanned spacecraft sent to explore part of the Solar System.

space shuttle Reusable spacecraft with wings. It carries astronauts between Earth and a space station and also takes satellites into space and brings them back again.

sulphuric acid An oily liquid that can dissolve some substances.

terraforming Changing a planet so that it is more like Earth.

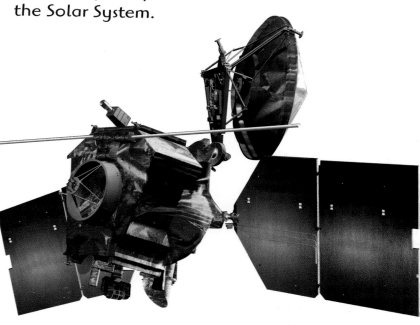

Index

WEBFINDER

http://www.bbc.co.uk/science/space/solarsystem/mercury/index.shtml

http://www.bbc.co.uk/science/space/solarsystem/venus/index.shtml

http://www.bbc.co.uk/science/space/solarsystem/earth/index.shtml

http://www.bbc.co.uk/science/space/solarsystem/mars/index.shtml

http://mars.jpl.nasa.gov/funzone_flash.html

http://dustbunny.com/afk/planets/mercury

http://kidsastronomy.com/venus.htm

http://www.esa.int/esaKIDSen/Earth.html

GRAHAM, Ian

The near
planets